# BAD ADVICE

## A BOOK OF POEMS ABOUT BROKENNESS, DEFEAT AND CONQUER.

## SARA L WARD

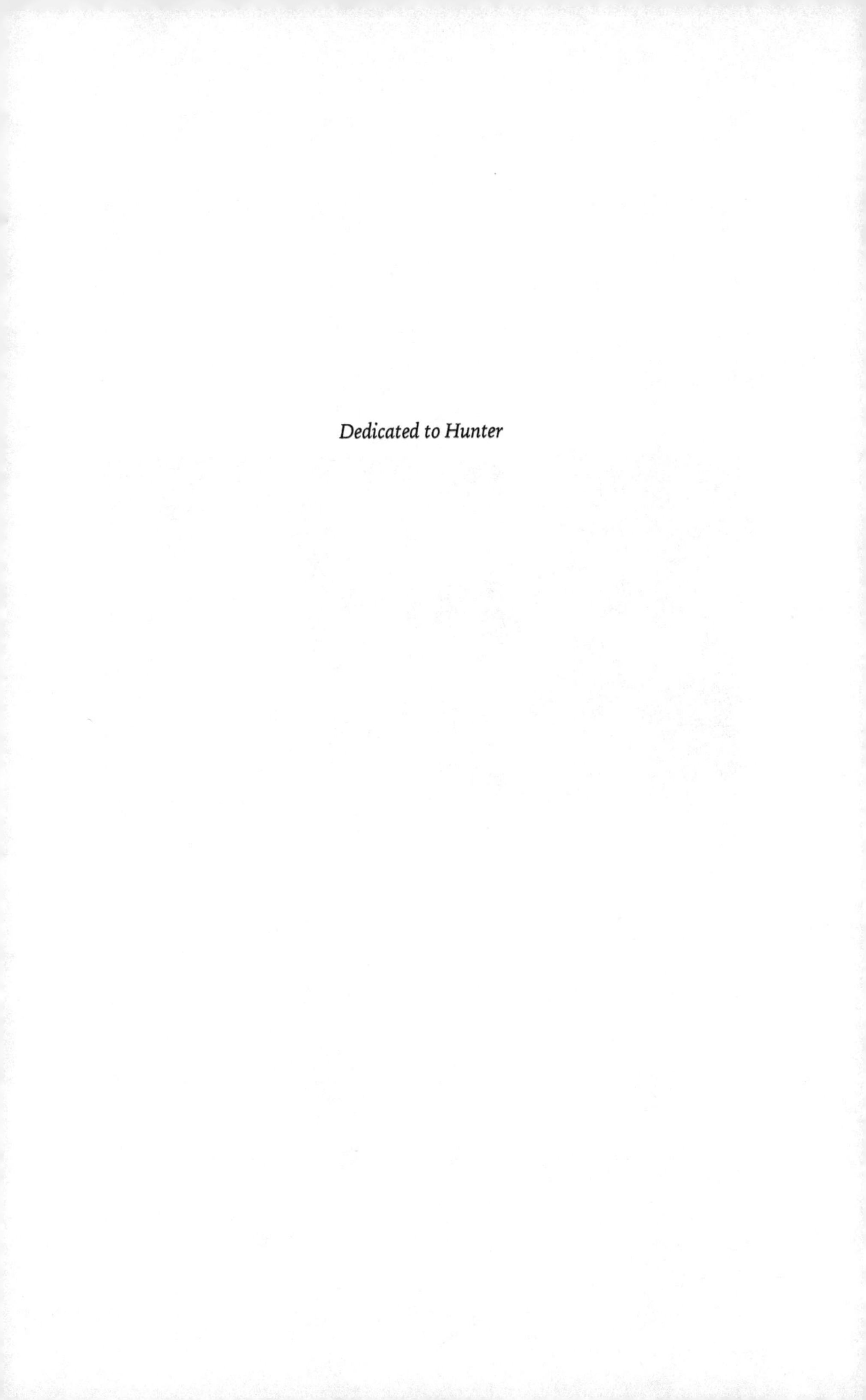

*Dedicated to Hunter*

# HUNTER

Hunter, my dear little brother
we might not have been blood
but there was love like no other
the true definition of a gentle giant
no need for greed, no need for defiance
you had everything in front of you
but it's the silent hell that took you
we'll never be the same
but I'm glad you're no longer filled with pain

and when our hearts are breaking
there's no way of faking the pain we feel inside
and I know you wouldn't want us to cry
you'd say shut up I'm just a guy
but you were more than that
you were so fly
you had the best kind of style
the best kind of smile
the best kind of hugs
I can't believe you've been gone for only a little while

And now we're left here
trying not to hear the truth
but it's inescapable now
they've shown us the proof
All I can hope for is that your soul will rest for eternity
and you'll stay right by us, never deserting
we'll love you forever, no matter the hurting

I love you Hunter
may you rest in peace

1998-2018

# TABLE OF CONTENTS

# PROLOGUE

Let me start off by saying that I have a great life now. I am grateful for the support that I have and that I wasn't tossed aside by the ones that really matter. I have a life that I can be proud of when I honestly thought that would never happen.

I've gone through some deep, dark shit that wasn't easy for me to wrap my head around. I have searched far within myself to pull out the good that was left behind all the broken glass inside. I lost years off my life for not understanding sooner, but it was a battle I had to wage with myself.

This book is something that I have worked on for many years. It has been in the back of my brain for what feels like an eternity. It is absolutely crazy how difficult it is to write about my experiences and how it makes me feel.

I have always thought I would need to explain the background of my poetry and I guess, in a way, I still feel that need to place some kind of context as to why I write what I write. I don't want to explain further than I am, as it makes my stomach and throat want to rip out of body. My hands and arms don't feel attached to the rest of me; and my mind is so conflicted as to why I would want to destroy its work of all the hiding and protecting it has done.

I've wanted to be a published author for as long as I can remember. I didn't care what genre it was going to be, I just wanted to see my writings in print with a dedicated ISBN. I want to smell that freshly printed book and cry on it. This whole process has been so emotional, and I can't believe I'm finally going to release it.

I started writing poetry and short stories when I was in elementary school. I honestly do not know why but it has always been there. I use poetry as a coping mechanism. It makes me feel something and it gets my feelings out of my head and body. I tuck it away for the days when I need extra reminders that I'm okay now.

Some of my poems are even little songs in my head. I am not a singer, *at all,* but they just end up having their own tune sometimes.

I decided to set this book in the 5 Stages of Grief because although I have lost way too many people, I believe those stages relate to any type of trauma. When you go through a tragic event you will go through all of those stages: Denial, Anger, Bargaining, Depression and Acceptance. They don't even obey the same line up or time frame. It's not like you go through these stages in a row, they can be thrown at you at any time. It's a cycle that you have to go through to live.

I was sexually assaulted when I was eight years old. I will not be going into detail about it because it's too painful for me to talk about. So much so that I didn't tell anyone for 15 years, not my parents, no family, no friends. Not a single person knew what had happened to me. I went about my life like a normal child the best that I could. It wasn't until I was 23 years old after a night of drinking with my boyfriend of a year (who is my husband now and I cherish him in so many ways) asked me how many men I had slept with.

This triggered something in me and it made me want to explain for the first time in my life the reason I had been promiscuous and how my childhood trauma had affected the rest of my life. By the time I finally said the words out loud, my pain had surfaced in other ways.

I had already made several attempts to end my life between the ages of 18 and 20. I had no desire or will to live. I moved out of my parents' house the week after I graduated high school and moved in with a few roommates for the summer. When that fell through, I moved into my own apartment. I had a boyfriend that I stayed with sometimes and friends to hang out with. All we did was get drunk and high, but I still felt very alone.

I went to community college for a year and then transferred to Savannah College of Art and Design to study fashion design.

From the outside, it was a dream plan. I was set to be a fashion designer. I was supposed to move to New York or LA to study top labels and build my own brand, but I couldn't do it. My brain was so messed up that I would isolate myself in a room at a school building in the middle of the night. I would cry a lot and try to call my parents who didn't understand why I was feeling the way that I did. For me, everything was boiling up and I was at a breaking point.

When I was nineteen, I met my ex-husband. He was a few years older and stationed outside of Savannah. He had already been divorced from his first wife and they had a son together. We got married just two months after my 20th birthday and had only been together for not even eight months, six months of that he was in Iraq.

His parents lived in Arizona at the time, so I flew out to see him during his two-week R&R. We stayed with his parents and had plans of getting married during that time. I did not notify my parents until two days before the wedding to fly out if they wanted to see me get married. We drove from Arizona to Vegas and had a small wedding where we were married by an Elvis impersonator.

The night before the wedding and the days following afterwards were hell for me, but I was determined to stay with him. Our relationship had been violent from the start; I felt like I had finally found the person who could kill me.

He was deployed for another six months and during that time I quit school and moved from Savannah to Charlotte to be closer to my family. When he came home, he decided he wanted to go back to Savannah for a few weeks to see his friends. He left and I was devastated.

It was then that I was admitted into a psych ward and held for eight days. I had my faults, I'm not perfect, but it was a place I never want to go to again.

After that, our relationship continued in a dysfunctional and abusive way for another year with him being sent to jail for a week on assault charges. Even still, we stayed together for several more months. When we eventually separated and got divorced, I felt relief but also failure.

It wasn't until some of my old friends and my family brought me back to life. Since then, I have been on a journey of healing, and it has not been easy in any sense. Along the road I have lost my beloved brother-in-law to suicide, and it has killed me and my husband every day since. I wish I could have saved him and told him my story and helped show him how to survive. It will be a regret that I have for the rest of my life.

I was too afraid to talk about my experiences because it's taboo, it's not meant to be brought up and not meant to be seen but that's fucked up in itself. I didn't create this trauma, this trauma created me and who I am today. I have to live with it so I'm the one who has to be comfortable with it, not everyone else.

Before I even really started to try to heal, I could not see through the darkness. I just thought that that was how it was supposed to be; that there was no escape from the walls that my life had created.

I only have flashes of images from my assault. I don't know how my brain was able to kick it out of my mind. I guess I didn't fully understand it and I think it was my mind's way of controlling it for my sanity. I've internalized everything my whole life and have tried to make each thought go through a process.

A therapist told me once that it's okay to be triggered. It's just how you react to those triggers that make the difference in whether you move forward or backwards. Some days I move forward and some days it feels like I'm years behind again, but the point is to keep moving. Keep trying. Be kind to yourself first and always.

I am a complicated person, I know this, but at the same time I'm alive. I'm at a place now where I can even write a little bit of my story and release my poetry and my words. I have hope that I can help another person. Maybe just one person to not feel so alone. That there is another side to the darkness. You just have to reach for it and keep trying.

My hope is that anyone reading this will find within themselves compassion, strength, and openness. It takes real power to pull yourself out of an abyss. I feel that there is only one life to live so we might as well try our best to see the beauty life has to offer because we have to survive. We have to get through this trauma and these traumatic events. We have to find a place in this world and find something that makes us feel alive. We have to fight for ourselves and make the demons in our heads go away because everyone has a right to find love. Not just with other people but with themselves.

This is a tale of a girl who had to rise from the dead. So, from my mind to yours, I give you my life and poetry about brokenness, defeat, and conquer.

# BAD ADVICE

# PART ONE
### DENIAL

### DRINKING TILL I CRY

Drinking till I cry
all my friends ask
but I can't tell them why
keeping my secrets hidden
wondering if anyone will find
the real me hidden deep inside

### PARANOIA

I live in a state of paranoia
and I know it's not right
I'm not trying to annoy you
I'm just along for the ride

Some days I'm on fire
but then I walk my days on a wire
Maybe I'm just tired
or maybe I'm waiting on this to backfire
or maybe I'm just lonely again

My fear paralyzes me
I'm thinking they should sterilize me
the fear rolls through me
and then I think I'm through it
but then the fear rolls through me again

I keep reliving all my sins
I beg and beg for it to end
but it seems this never ends
dragging through the river bend
it seems I'm being tortured
maybe I should build a fortress
to save me from myself

## LIES

I tell lies to hide what's going on inside
these walls are driving me to oblivion
it's all I got to not bang my head against the floor
they say tell me more, tell me more
what are you really here for?
I told them I was fine
but they can hear me crying
I told them they were blind
but they can see me lying

## AFRAID

I spent my days wondering how to deal
I spent my days wondering if it's real
but the truth is there's no way to feel any different
there's no way to rewind a thing like that
there's no way to feel like you're not trapped
there's no way to get out of your own mind
it keeps coming back and it attacks you
but as long as you have someone to cry to
it'll all be worth it, the hell can't find you

sometimes I think it's a good thing
to obsess and compress that thing inside you
until it explodes and there's no one left beside you
it's a dark and twisted world to live in
but sometimes it's the only way to get through
the pain that's trapped inside you

I'm not saying do as I do
I've not reached my end and I never will
but only time will tell
whether I'm meant for heaven or hell

I'm just trying to say
I'm not afraid
even if I have to tell myself that
a million times over
again
and again
and again

## We All Fall Down

There once was a girl who ruled the world
and all of her disciples followed
they were in awe of her
and all her worth
and the rest fell behind and wallowed
but along the path the girl was broken
all alive and hell awoken
she went down and all around
searching far and wide
near and behind
with nothing ever spoken

She searched for answers
it was like a cancer
spinning around like a ball dancer
dancing through time
trying her best to rewind
but nothing ever happened

Instead it festered and grew
and she became someone no one knew
that's what happens
when you're trapped in the memories
and all you want is soliloquy
but nothing ever happens

## I Don't Know Why

I don't know why
but it's all the time
it goes over and over in my mind
like a record that's spinning out of control
I'm a woman with a broken soul

And I don't know why
but it's summertime
so everything's fine in the city
where lovers meet
can you feel it?
it's in the air everywhere

And I don't know why
but I'm praying for peace of mind
so if anyone is out there
please hear me
cause I'm praying to anyone who will listen
before my mind tells me different

And I don't know why
it's all the time
but it's summertime
so everything's fine in the city

WHERE THE DEVIL ROAMS

Looking for safety on your couch
all my belongings in my favorite pouch
can't go home
where the devil roams

## Hypocrisy

The moon
the stars
the hypocrites aren't very far
I hope they come back soon

star light
star bright
I hope they all come out tonight
cause we've got to grind until we lose sight
spinning like crazy on the floor
I keep coming back for more
across the hypocritical sky

we were beautiful
but I can see the fire in your eyes
you're full of hypocrisy
you're full of lies
I can see the sickness in your eyes

You say I'm the one to ruin it all
but you don't see the pain you've caused
to the ones who haunt you for the daily cause
they say they know why you fight for all
cause your fist is swinging for the wrong king of them all

So we sing for the condemned
is this love that we need to mend?
or is it my pride that I need to defend?
either way, I know that I'm one of the condemned.

So, I just look up at
the moon
the stars
I know the hypocrites aren't very far
I hope they come back soon

### What Happens In Vegas

They say what happens in Vegas
stays in Vegas
but that's not what the marriage license says

Elvis is singing his best blue suede shoes
I'm walking down the aisle
thinking I should probably run
but before I know it, it's already done
and now I'm wrapped up in my own blues

The night before was hell
running all around the hotel
looking for you
while you're looking for someone new

Elvis is singing his best blue suede shoes
I'm walking down the aisle
thinking I should probably run
but before I know it, it's already done
and now I'm wrapped up in my own blues

I found you drinking in the casino
told you it's time to come back
The yelling begins
The cops are called
The neighbors can hear our fight
I just can't make this right

They say what happens in Vegas
stays in Vegas
but that's not what the marriage license says

## I BOUGHT A GUN

I bought a gun in the back alley of my mind
I didn't know that I'd want it all the time
I wasted away
told the cops not to stay
but I wished quietly
they'd take you away

"Shh be quiet
don't say a word
It's not like your voice
will ever be heard

they won't do nothing
it was only roughing
I'll be better tomorrow
you can quit the sorrow"

I bit my tongue
even though I just wanted to run
but now I'm too tired
running from the sun
I fought it off
told myself I'm done

Oh great
here it comes
another fight
another time
another day
another fine
another stay
another rhyme
another world gone mad

### No Sense

It's probable
it's plausible
it's completely and utterly logical
but it still doesn't make sense to me

# PART TWO
## ANGER

**OH, PEOPLE**

Oh, people
they really fuck you up sometimes
they can make you feel
like you've lost your mind
but people come and go
that's fine

oh, people
they can make you cry
they can make you smile
but that's really only every once in awhile
but people come and go
it's wild

oh, people
if they only knew
what it is we could do
but they don't have a clue
but people come and go
it's fine

## Aggressive

Found out I need to be aggressive
if I want to be progressive
please God don't let me get arrested
my nerves are getting tested

my ears have been ringing
your words have lost their meaning
please let me say I'm leaving
oh no, don't pretend you're grieving
please let me say goodbye
I can't do this one more time

## Delirium

Now I just think that this is hilarious
you're gotten to the point where you're just delirious
all this talk is making me furious
move along before I make this serious

## LOADED GUN

Held a loaded gun
thought it might be fun
to blow it all away
crying in the night
shook up from the fight
but that's okay cause I'm going to smoke it all away anyway

I can hear you say now
you'll amount to nothing
you learn something new every day
I can hear you say now
you'll amount to nothing
you learn something new every day

all of the fights and all of the frights
wouldn't make me leave that night
shaking until you're out of sight
but that's okay cause I'm going to fool you anyway

I can hear you say now
you won't amount to nothing
you learn something new every day
I can hear you say now
you won't amount to nothing
you learn something new every day

you broke my heart
but I can't wait for us to part
pack your bags quick get on your way
I'm looking for a new start
I don't know if I can do it without your part
but that's okay cause I'm going to do it my way anyway

I can hear you say now
you won't amount to nothing
you learn something new every day
I can hear you say now
you won't amount to nothing
you learn something new every day

# BAD ADVICE

I've got my gun,
now turn out the light
you better run boy
it's not my night
but that's okay cause I'm going to get a new man anyway

### KNOCK 'EM DEAD

They'll never understand
your words are spinning in my head
they're twisting and hissing
they're trying to get me
doing my best to resist
but they're creeping all in my bed

so I'm just going to do them a favor
and knock 'em dead
yeah I'm just going to knock 'em dead
knock knock knock 'em dead

## 4 AM

By the fourth hour
I've got my eye on you
so pour me another whiskey sour
before I say, "can I go home with you?"

come on now show me what you can do
hey baby I can be your little lady
but I swear to God
don't fucking call me crazy

It's 4 AM
and I'm not doing well
so just give me something to pass the time
I already know I'm going to hell

so come on now show me what you can do
cause I've got nothing really better to do
let's get a little lost
but remember I'm the boss
I can be your little lady
but I swear to God
don't fucking call me crazy

## THE DEVIL & ME

Don't get too close
cause you won't like what you see
I've been speaking with the devil
and he keeps telling me,
"Why don't you come down here
and live by the sea
It's filled with fire as far as the eye can see."
I say, "No fiend not this week
but we'll see when the moon comes out again."
He says, "Come on now you know you're going to sin
so why don't you just go ahead and give in."
And that's when I know that it's all going to begin
I'm set for the stage that I'm going to have to defend

Oh my oh my
can you see me?
Oh my oh my I think I'm going
Oh my oh my I think I'm going down
to the sea of fire is where I'll be found
flames as high as the eye can see
it's the only place that can really set me free
the devil and me for eternity
the devil and me in eternity
the devil and me live in eternity

## GUN SLINGER

He had liquor on his lips
guns slinging on his hips
my name dripping from his lips
I fell hard for him
he had me tight around his grip
but I won't let it happen again

he's a gun slinger
a dead ringer
he put diamonds on my ring finger
but I know, I know, I know now
he's the grim reaper
he may walk the walk
and talk the talk
but all he does is balk
at the notion of causing commotion
he thinks he's sly but I'll tell him why
we need to set this plan in motion
you can run as fast as you can
but I've got guns now too
they call me the gun slinger
and I'm a dead ringer
when I put the trigger on my ruby red finger

## Hit Me

You hit me
you apologize
it gets me every time
so let's turn back time
and hit rewind

I hit you
I apologize
I get you every time
so let's turn back time
and hit rewind

So hit me if you would
this time why don't you make it last for good
cause I've just got to get out of this hood
so please hit me if you could

I don't want to hear your bullshit
I'm through covering for your ass
in fact I'm through with it all
I hope they lock you up for good
and somebody fucks you in the ass
so please hit me if you could

## I'M HERE TO TELL YOU

You think you're bad
you think you're cool
you think that you've already won
but I'm here to tell you
that the battle's just begun
so grab your keys
grab your head
grab what you'll need when you're dead
cause I'm here to tell you
that you better fucking run
you think it's clear
you think it's dear
you think that I am nowhere near
but I'm here to tell you
that my words have been sincere
so grab a beer and hold tight
cause you'll need it when I'm done
I'm coming for you
and there's nothing you can do
you already blew it
when you thought you knew it
you're a liar trapped
wrapped in a web of disease
I've come to unleash
if you'll have me please
I'm here to tell you
I don't need your permission
to put you in submission
so close your eyes and say goodbye
you won't recover from this condition

## POISON TO YOUR CURE

I'm the poison to your cure
I keep begging for more and more
I don't know what the hell I'm really here for
but I keep coming back for more and more

I guess I'm just going to have to lure
cause I'm the poison ivy to your wretched skin
you thought that I only slept with you then?
I'm going to sneak in until it all seeps in
cause I'm the poison to your cure

Let's see how you deal with it then
cause I'm the kudzu to your hateful self
you can break me down but I'll always rise
especially when I get liquor from the top shelf
and as my beauty grows stronger
I'll be proud of myself
cause I'm going to sneak in until it all seeps in
cause I'm the poison to your cure

## CITY OF RUINS

Ruining you has been really fun
all night I've been waiting on the sun
cause when it rises I'm going to have to run
making you my enemy
is the best thing for my memory
cause I'm a fucking wild card
you never know what I'm going to do
but you're in it now, you're fucking screwed

I created the City of Ruins
terror can make you really cruel
I won't be your little fool
turning me into something I can't control
so pour them some of that stuff that I'm brewing
and put them in the place I call the City of Ruins

Welcome to the freak show
I'm going to pull you in
cause when I'm done I'll know all your sins
gather up all your favorite friends
and tell them you'll never see them again
cause I'm a fucking wild card
you never know what I'm going to do
but you're in it now, you're fucking screwed

I created the City of Ruins
anger can make you break all your rules
so I'm going to make the rejects look like fools
turn them into ridiculed mules
pour them some of that stuff I've been brewing
and put them in the place I call the City of Ruins

now you're in love
but you don't know I do this just for fun

## I Can't Do This Anymore

I can't do this anymore
quit calling me a whore
that shit has gotten crazy
get the fuck off the couch, lazy

bitch get a job
the Army doesn't owe you nothing
do what you got to do, if you got to rob
so quit doing all the puffing
and go get the dogs
don't think that I'm bluffing
when I call the cops

I used to think that I could go the mile
this pairing is hard work
wipe that look off your face
I hate that fucking smirk
all you do is sit and smile
so tell the county clerk
annul it without a trace
get your fucking shit out
I'm overworked

**DONE**

Faces
Places
Left are the traces
None that they can see
Who am I to defy
The good graces of the glorified
The army set you up to be

I've heard the things
Your friends have done
They're just like you
Look at you
Now you're done

LIVE

The fuck I didn't give
I did it so I could live
what do you want for me
I've given all I can give
I did it so I could live

39

# PART THREE
## BARGAINING

# BAD ADVICE

## LAUGH IN THE FACE OF DANGER

I laughed in the face of danger
I felt safety in the arms of strangers
I know I put my life in danger
but at the time life couldn't have been stranger

there are days when I can wish it all away
my eyes are open and I can breathe again
feeling the air seeping in,
lingering and tinkering at the thoughts that take me away

then it creeps in again and I feel my days are numbered
ringing in my ears like a roaring thunder
I don't know why I can't be stronger
I try to push it away but I couldn't have been wronger
I screwed up and it blew up
now I'm left with years I can't remember
going on an endless bender
I'm at the end of my rope, standing on a downward slope
cut me open and salt my wounds
let me know when it's all over
hopefully it'll be over soon

I need to remind myself
I can do it all by myself
I don't need anyone to tell me how to be
I have it all hidden deep inside of me
I just laugh in the face of danger
I can dance through life and maybe meet a nice stranger
I'm the realest of the real, I'm the real game changer
I can steal away time, I'll make you feel like you're mine
but just know this, with me you'll live your life in danger

my mind is always racing
I gotta keep myself from pacing
I'm trying to stay grounded
but I'd rather be chasing
these foul remarks away

# BAD ADVICE

let me go I'm on my way
feel like I'm crazy
but you've made my day
dancing the night away
laughing it all away
I just laugh in the face of danger

44

## If They Only Knew

When the wind blows
everyone will know
everything slows
but if you only knew
how I got the blues
you would cry the same tears
you would have the same fears
you would cry to the heavens
with the same kind of cheers

## The Basement

I step down
so I don't drown
I just bring it to the basement
to wrap my head around
I freak out
so I don't doubt
all the hard work I've done
I need to get it out
then I'll run as fast as I can
it's scary what's hiding around
if they find me out
then they'll know then I'm done
I have to keep it in the basement
trying to find my placement
it's a deep hole
it'll swallow me whole
if I allow it to
but I'm not breaking soon
I just need to scream
live out all my dreams
drown out all the schemes
life isn't all it seems
sometimes you need to just scream
and leave it in the basement
with all your broken dreams

## DOWN ON RIVER STREET

Down on River Street
I can hear the beat
of the saxophone at play
he's drinking whiskey's neat
while collecting his thoughts down at the bay
saying, "Goddamn it's hot out today"

the trees are swaying
all the kids are playing
I don't have anywhere left to go

Down on River Street
where the candy is so sweet
and the magic shop is selling disguises
I can see the birds flying high on the horizon
Bar hopping, enjoying those liquor treats
with tattoos heavy on the Army elite

the trees are swaying
all the kids are playing
I don't have anywhere left to go

Down on River Street
where the night never fleets
and the bars are filled with stars
we're making deals on the dance floor trying to be discreet
but damn I gotta get these heels off my aching feet

right off MLK boulevard
the night before weighing heavy

the trees are swaying
all the kids are playing
I don't have anywhere left to go

### RED, WHITE & BLUE

Red lips,
white lies
and blue skies.
Vegas trips,
liquor wise
and long goodbyes.
Jaded scripts,
sad eyes
and on the brink of demise.

But I've got red, white and blue.
yeah I've got red, white and blue
Red lips,
white lies,
and I've got blue skies.

I'm going to take a trip down memory lane
nothing can ever really be sane
there will always be things that I'm going to fear
but now the road seems pretty fucking clear

I've got red, white and blue.
yeah I've got red, white and blue
Red lips,
white lies,
and I've got blue skies.

## CRUEL TO ME

We live reckless
you buy me sweet necklaces
when you make me cry
why do you lie
what can I do to make you like me
we fight every night
I want to be happy
but that's too sappy for you
what can I do
you're no fool
but you're cruel to me

You don't want to lose me
I'm a diamond in the rough
and if that's not enough
I'll make you want me
oh baby taunt me
you know you want to
but you're cruel to me

## FORGIVE ME

Father, forgive me for I have sinned
for I know not what I do
but I know that if it were up to me
I would creep around where I'm not supposed to
I would stay up late every night
And dream about the summer rights
With the air as thick as the city lights
roses in my hair, living free without a care

So forgive me
for I can't see
without a little crazy inside of me
it's all I need
when I'm losing sight of me
it sets me free, it sets me free

Father, forgive me for I have tried
to move past the nights that I cried
for I know not what I do
but I know that if it were up to me
I would dance under the silver moon
and hike up my skirt for a little fun
with the boys as bad as a hired gun
hands in the air, living free without a care

So forgive me
for I can't see
without a little crazy inside of me
it's all I need
when I'm losing sight of me
it sets me free, it sets me free

## How Would I Know

How would I know
what was I supposed to do
if you only knew
the hell that we've been through
you wouldn't ask those questions
you wouldn't make those vague assumptions
you wouldn't put up a fight
you would know that's not right
to leave a girl broken
her thoughts now awoken
all it does is fester
quarrels up inside
screaming how long can I test her
is she dead inside
it hides and I can't find
where it ends and I begin
so do me a favor
don't ask why I defend
cause how would I know
I just played pretend

## What Does It Mean

I said God what does it mean
when I'm praying on my knees
I just can't understand why you put me on this earth
I try so hard to look up with ease
but it's all I've got when it's all been too much
I say God what does it mean

I said I can swing a hammer
but I think it might put me in the slammer
so God tell me what to do
when he says I'm coming for you
God what does it mean

I said I can't take it back
so you might as well just turn right back
cause I'm too far gone
I wished so hard that the battle was won
but I know that I can't win this one
so God what does it mean

They say everything happens for a reason
but I'm beginning to think that this is treason
I know the cops won't do a thing
so I just look up to the king
and say God what does it mean

## A Sinner's World

Death can consume you
it walks up and down your spine
sets the tone
and then it moves you
you become wrapped until you're trapped
in the memories that soothe you
they can be dark and remarkable
they can be bright but that's not marketable
whatever you do don't walk towards the light
it's a sinner's world and it seems we're losing sight
of the difference between wrong and right
we move in a sense
but what's the difference
it's screwed up, it doesn't make sense
we're left to our own accords

## A Different Place

I sent my mind to a different place
I knew if I didn't I would only see your face
now I'm walking in a different pace
to save myself from the falling grace

## Rain

I ran out in the pouring rain
you would think that they couldn't hear me complain
but I cried to the heavens, it was all in vain
the sky opened up and they said my name
I crashed on to the floor thinking I was insane
they came out like they had before
they spoke so sweet and tried to explain
but all I could think of was their game

it's the unknown that's the worst
it's the begging that makes this a curse
it's the unknown that's the worst
it's the begging that makes this a curse

I told them I couldn't take anymore
why do you do this why is it all a mess
show me how you're going to change
tell me how it won't be the same
then I'll know that we've settled the score
but they laughed and said they'll give me more
I thought that I was done but as I looked around
I saw that I was going underground

it's the unknown that's the worst
it's the begging that makes this a curse
it's the unknown that's the worst
it's the begging that makes this a curse

It was a longing that I've had before
the sky was falling at my door
they heard my cries and wiped my tears
told me "darling, don't you live in fear
the sky may fall and the sun will fade
but I'm sure that you'll be okay
along the path is where you'll see me
in the open field when you need me"

# BAD ADVICE

don't leave my side I started to scream
who else will I confide
you were gone I looked around
I screamed for you but there was no sound
don't leave me I cried as I fell to my knees

it's the unknown that's the worst
it's the begging that makes this such a curse

## UGLY CRY

Sometimes
I ugly cry
and it can last for hours
and hours turn to weeks
and
It's something I don't want to repeat
but
It's like a crashing wave
that takes your breath away
pulls you under
until it's all you wonder
see the lightening strike
hear the thunder

The noise can be deafening
almost like a reckoning
I fear for myself
for others
is this my only destiny?
I have to get a grip
I can't go on this trip
I try to pretend
there's nothing I can't handle
but sometimes
I just want to ugly cry

### Dissolve

I've cried a lot
I've fought a lot
and frankly
I'm fucking tired a lot
and sometimes
I can't fight through it
and
I've tried
I've really fucking tried
but
I can't help it
I want to unwind in it
I want to climb in it
I want it to rear it's fucking ugly head
so I can bring up the dead
and let my emotions try to survive it
I want to fight it
I want to hide it
I want it to clear a path
so I can bring on the wrath
and let my fear divide it
all in all
I try not to fall
but sometimes
I can't help but
to
dissolve

# PART FOUR
## DEPRESSION

## The Path To Paradise Begins In Hell

The path to paradise begins in hell
do your best to wish me well
I've gone deeper than the darkest well
you thought you knew but you couldn't tell
my mind traps secrets like the darkest hell
I tried to get out but you couldn't help
I've gone deeper than the darkest hell
I tried to get out but you couldn't tell

## INSANE

Sitting in the rain
I feel like I'm going insane
yeah I feel like I'm going insane
yeah I feel like I'm going insane

Nothing left of me that remains
you took it all I'll never be the same
I wasn't meant for you anyway
even though I can't forget the things you say
pounding it deeper and deeper, I don't need a repeater
but you can't always get your way
you really need to clean up your demeanor
you're letting everyone see you're crazy
they'll know your secrets, like that you're fucking lazy
but you can't always get your way

so I'm just sitting in the rain
I feel like I'm going insane
yeah I feel like I'm going insane
yeah I feel like I'm going insane

Feeling the battle go on and on
I don't know which side I'm on
they've both been stringing me along
can't tell right from wrong
it all just keeps going on and on
grabbing a hold of me, I don't know where I belong
I don't know why I can't just move on
my heads spinning, my vision's blurry
I feel like my life is in such a hurry
it's making me sick, it's making me worry

so I'm just sitting in the rain
yeah I feel like I'm going insane
yeah I feel like I'm going insane

## AFFIRMATIONS & CONFIRMATIONS

She's made out of affirmations and confirmations
old rhymes and wild times
she needs satisfaction and lots of traction
you can't tame a woman like that

she's on a mission
and she's always wishing
that you'd love her like that
but it's unknown
when we're thrown
you can't see the way she acts

oh my what a rush
to touch a vine of poison
call the boys in
lets bring the noise in
it's time to rid us
of the reason and the treason

oh wouldn't you like to know
just how it goes
the stories keep scrolling
and just then
when you didn't think
it's gone in a blink
and now your world
is rolling away

## CORRIDOR

You said you need time to think
you've been going mad and you're on the brink
in the place where the sand never sinks
I said you've been gone a year
so, what am I supposed to do here?
but you didn't care
you just thought about your own fears

so I've got pills in one hand
a bottle in the other
I'm slipping further down
trying not to blow my cover
but I think I'll just drown
because I've got nothing else to live for

now I'm walking down the corridor
looking for my escape
but they've got guards at every door
see the people with sad eyes
I'm one of them
we've all lost our mind

I just wanted you to be happy and at peace
but you're gentle words were just a tease
we went back to the same place where the judge told us not to
being with you was a wild ride
for a moment I thought I had everything with you by my side
but it turns out you didn't care
you just thought about your own career

so I've got pills in one hand
a bottle in the other
I'm slipping further down
trying not to blow my cover
but I think I'll just drown
because I've got nothing else to live for

# BAD ADVICE

now I'm walking down the corridor
looking for my escape
but they've got guards at every door
see the people with sad eyes
I'm one of them
we've all lost our mind

down the corridor
down the corridor
down the corridor
I can't keep going
down the corridor

## SAD FOREVER

Little brother was meant for big things
he got sad and did some things
he didn't mean to hurt us
but it broke us in two

We'll be sad forever
without you, without you
at least we have each other

Life's dream is mean
we're lost and now you're free
wish you were here

You were a light in our world
now it's dark and we're in a whirl
you won't even get to meet our little girl
now it's dark and we're in a whirl
without you, without you here

little brother why did you leave
now all we can do is grieve
for you
cause you're gone

wish it wasn't like this
I know it's hard
but fuck this
I would give anything
to have you back would be a dream
but life's mean and we'll be sad forever
without you, without you here

## THAT DAY CHANGED ME

That day changed me
screaming I'm not an insurgent
I need a diversion

forever embedded in my head
when he held me down on the bed
black and blued my eyes until I couldn't see
that's when I lost all of me
no hope for the road
there's too much of a heavy load

proclamations aren't around here
declarations won't appear
cause there's nothing left of me here

no words to express
when you can't even get dressed
that day changed me

## OUR DEMISE

Our demise
is off to a good start
much to my surprise
I'm good at breaking hearts
see the angel in disguise
helping them out with my demise

I need to figure out this mystery
I can't let this all be my history
don't let me wallow in my own misery
I can't let this all be my history

These feelings are coming over me
this shit is going to drive me crazy
I can feel it all crushing me
the future looks so very hazy
dreams I can no longer foresee
I can feel this all coming over me

I need to figure out this mystery
I can't let this all be my history
don't let me wallow in my own misery
I can't let this all be my history

Saying this is just the world we live in
can I get a helping hand?
I just don't think that I can give in
this isn't what I had planned
I really need my heart to stop crippling
I'm going to try to let it all sink in

I need to figure out this mystery
I can't let this all be my history
don't let me wallow in my own misery
I can't let this all be my history

## Pain

A pain so deep
it can't make it to the surface
until it's dark
and I'm alone
and I have to close the curtains
the pain is deep
I can feel it coming for me
it's messing up my sleep

## YEAH I CRIED

Yeah I cried
thinking about the night
when I almost died
no end in sight
and now the walls are closing in

I can see their faces
by God's good graces
please tell me how to help them
don't let the mayhem take them

got me strapped to this table
please tell me this is some kind of fable
the doctors all in white
please tell me I don't have to fight
and now the walls are closing in

I can see their faces
by God's good graces
please tell me how to help them
don't let the mayhem take them

grabbing my head
trying to shake off what they're telling me
I just wish I was dead
please don't let these pills take over me
and now the walls are closing in

I can see their faces
by God's good graces
please tell me how to help them
don't let the mayhem take them

## ANGELS

Angel from the sky above
what are you thinking of, my love
I wish you could come down here
or I could go up there

please forgive me
for the lies I told
I didn't mean to cause the trouble
I don't know what becomes of me
my heart gets so cold sometimes
it takes control over me

angels from the skies above
please watch over me
I need your guidance from the violence
I can't do it without your love

## I HAVEN'T BEEN MYSELF

I haven't been myself
I don't know what that is yet
cause I don't know myself
but we're all just trying to find ourselves
and sometimes it's really hard
when you're trying your very best
but I'm willing and able
to give my troubles to the angels
I'm willing and able
to break my fears over this table
cause I've got to run now
from these painful labels
cause I won't make it
if I keep listening to these fables
I'm willing and able
to give my troubles to the angels

I haven't been myself for a while now
but I know, I know, I know now
I can't trust myself with these feelings that I have now
cause I'm willing and able
to give my troubles to the angels
can you please, can you please, can you please tell me how
cause I can't shake these feelings that I have now
is this the end, is this the end, is this the end now?
cause I'm willing and able
to give my troubles to the angels

### Her

Driving off down the gravel road
the sky's so dim and the wind just swings
she thinks that she's going on a whim
but she doesn't know that she can't swim
it pulls her down brings her in to the grim
if she keeps this up then you know he'll win

but
I would be lying
if I didn't say
she reminds me so much of myself that it's insane
seeing her fight what's going on inside
reminds me when I almost lost my mind
they're all screaming
it's all around there is no escape
I could drown in the noise
I almost forgot what it was like
to live in a world that destroys
I lost so much that I was banned
I know that you wouldn't understand
but all I could think of was the fall

When I look into her eyes
I see a past that's filled with lies
they scream loud and pierce through my skin
screeching for peace that's held from within
leaves me in a shallow grave

**74**

## BLACK

I try to look past the memories
but everything is black
I stay trapped in the memories
and I know I can't go back
but everything is revolving around an open door
I try to run through it but it shocks me to my core
electric currents run through my every being
how much more can I take, I'm just a human being

I look for a heavy vessel
to end my somber ways
I know I shouldn't think about
that dark and fateful day
but it's something I can't wrestle
I fight it every day

### Angels In Demand

There are angels in demand
It's getting out of hand
I'm getting out of my head
Help me now
They want me some how
Because there are
Angels in demand
It's getting out of hand
And I'm getting out of my head

## Drumming Away In Heaven

You let the devil creep in
he brought you deeper within
got you searching for the darkest sins
scratching the walls don't let it come in

Now you're drumming away in Heaven
rocking out with the angels
show them what it's like to drum away your aggression
making your hands bleed until their painful
drumming away in Heaven
drumming away in Heaven
drumming away in Heaven

Your brokenness shows in the drugs that surround you
all tied up with the lies that bound you
your kind heart was lost to the world around you
all the rising pressure can really astound you

Now you're drumming away in Heaven
rocking out with the angels
show them what it's like to drum away your aggression
making your hands bleed until their painful
drumming away in Heaven
drumming away in Heaven
drumming away in Heaven

Now you've morphed into a beautiful butterfly
to remind your mother you're still around
when she's crying out her eyes
hoping and praying that one day you'll rise
but angels can't come back when they're busy
drumming away in Heaven
drumming away in Heaven
drumming away in Heaven

# BAD ADVICE

So much potential can carry you away
to a land of dreams meant for today
until he sweeps in and takes it all away
nothing left to do but follow him all the way
down the rabbit hole we go
down the rabbit hole we go
down the rabbit hole we go

Now you're drumming away in Heaven
rocking out with the angels
show them what it's like to drum away your aggression
making your hands bleed until their painful
drumming away in Heaven
drumming away in Heaven
drumming away in Heaven

RIP Tony
1988-2012

## There Once Was A Girl

There once was a girl
in a lonely world
with a ribbon in her curls
and her life in a whirl
she wished for death
and one last breath
and for her dark knight
to take the kitchen knife
and slit her throat for good

### What Have I Done

I look for a release
but it never comes
this sickness weighs a ton
oh my, what have I done
I just wanted to have a little fun
it's a screwed up world
I'm just dying in it

80

## Silence

We suffer in silence
We suffer out loud
We suffer with violence
We push it all down

# BAD ADVICE

**MIRANDA**

I'll never forget your laugh
and the good times we used to have
and how much love you had for everyone
but yourself
you let yourself go
and couldn't hold your head high
trying to stay high all the time
just to forget the ones we've lost
but at what cost
will the pain stop
my tears have dried
but I'm still fighting them
caught up in the pain
I can't believe we're here again
I've lost a friend

1986 - 2020

## AGAIN

Watch the scene unfold
and let the truth be told

we weren't ready for it

but I guess

you never really are

We feel so far from the beginning
but then it feels so close again
replays through our heads again
crying, pounding our heads again

Reliving the pain
over
and
over
and
over
again.

## I Don't Know If You Would Have Done It

I don't know if you would have done it
if you could see how much we've cried for you
I don't know if you would have done it
if you could see how we'd die for you
it hurts still to know you're gone
forever lost
no one won

Maybe you're playing with Kobe
maybe you lucked out
skipped out on the pandemic
what a fucking mess we're in
your anxiety probably would have exploded
but now you're just floating
shooting pointers with a star
wish we could watch you
even from afar

I don't know if you would have done it
if you could see the kids
they're so big and full of life
you could have had your own
got a job, maybe a wife
settled down, made a life
but you chose a different route
now we're screwed up, covered in doubt
it's not your fault, I'll never blame
living this life it's a fucked up game
but come on, why the fuck are you not here anymore
couldn't you just have given us a little more
cause I don't know if you would have done it
if you could see the wreckage
see how much it's wrecked us
we'll never know
because you left us

84

## We Love Him Anyway

Our bodies tell a story
to remind them we're always grieving
never respect the leaving
love him anyway
even if he didn't want to stay
he left us before the time was up
we'll never give up
trying to learn the answers
it feels like a cancer
but we love him anyway

# BAD ADVICE

# PART FIVE
## ACCEPTANCE

# BAD ADVICE

## What Do You Expect

What do you expect
it wasn't easy
I've died a thousand times just to rise again
I've ran with the unwanted, the cons and the sleazy
I kept pulling myself back in
I never wanted it to be this way
but what do you expect
when your innocence is taken away

I've been through all the emotions
I've been broken
I've been wrecked
I've tried to hold devotion
I would sail the seven seas
if I thought it would heal me
but I know now
it'll always be a part of me
I've accepted this sickening fate
now I know what's really at stake

I've gone away
I've paid with days
I've heard all the things you've had to say
I can't let it happen again, no fucking way
pain isn't worth your freedom

so what do you expect
my life's a wreck
but at least I can suspect this is just the beginning
I've been pulled from the wreck
and I won't forget the hell I've been through
I believe in the power of myself
and what I can get through
it hasn't been easy
but what do you expect, life isn't just a run through

## ARTIST

I'm a goddamned artist
getting help from my dearly departed
watching over me is not for the fainthearted

now I'm feeling inspired
minds racing, I can't get tired
see the colors light up, they're all I admired
got to get money for when I'm retired

it's all upon us
I'm just trying to be honest
because I'm a goddess
yeah I'm a goddamned artist

feeling the angels all around me
they're following me
embracing me
never disgracing me

so hear me loud
and hear me proud
because I'm trying to tell you what it's all about

it's all upon us
I'm just trying to be honest
because I'm a goddess
yeah I'm a goddamned artist

## TASTELESS TREASURE

Tasteless treasure
yearly presents
endless amount of tears
you'll wish for the end
of everything, my friend
and wash it away with fear

I know what you're thinking
this life is sinking
endless amount of fears
you'll wish for the end
of everything, my friend
and wash it away with tears

The end is fine
if you believe in time
but my world is aching
don't trust the wine, it's not divine
if your heart is breaking like mine

The tide will come for everyone
you'll be ready, strong and steady
it'll take it's time
but you'll be just fine
when it gets too heavy

91

## A LITTLE BIT

I'm a little bit rock and roll
a little bit old school
a little bit heavy metal
and a whole lot of soul

## Wedding Day

Let's get married
and run away
we'll play the music from our wedding day
cause all I want to do is lay with you
in soft sheets made of rhythm and blues

we'll talk about our dreams, sing in regime
we'll live like the finest kings and queens
we'll shine under market lights and wild dreams

so baby, let's run away
we'll play the music from our wedding day
cause all I want to do is lay with you
in soft sheets made of rhythm and blues

all we'll think of are the ways
we can better the days
cause all there is do is make way
for the dreams of yesterday

we'll forget our sorrows
and live like there's no tomorrow
cause I feel safe with you
there's nothing that I'd rather do
than lay in soft sheets made of rhythm and blues

flowers in my hair
smoke blowing in the air
saying so long, humming our favorite tune
waiting for the ocean to grace us
we'll be on our honeymoon

## One Little Life

I told my friend you know what to do
tip it back and show us what to do
we'll go down the rabbit hole with you
tip it back and we'll go to the blue

One step down and you know what to do
tip it back and show us to the moon
one little drop will only do
we'll go down and show you what to do

I never win but that's not the point
you tip it back and smoke another joint
one little hit and you'll be fine
don't you worry, we've all lost our mind
there's nothing I wouldn't do for you
just tip it back and show me what to do

Forget the rest and follow the clues
one little life is all we can do
so live it up and tell me what to do
forget the rest and follow the clues

One little life is all we have
it didn't take much but that's all we had
my mind was lost along the way
I tripped up and it stayed the same
it didn't take much but that's all I had
one little life is all I have

## FOOL ME ONCE SHAME ON ME

I gave my demons too much power
they began to rule me
they're still swirling in my head
but I won't let them fool me
it's a hell of ride truly
you'd think so too if you only knew me
I've been through hell and back
so sue me
if I take you seriously
it's a new me

I shouldn't have let you take control
but you knew just how to play the role
you thought you could take my soul
but it comes with a price that'll take it's toll

fool me once shame on me
they tried to tell me but I couldn't see
blinded by the fire in my eyes
knocked me back down to size
but I rose through the fire
and I can't deny
I'm stronger than ever
I've been brought to a new life

95

## THE WORST IS OVER

I find a man
and we fall in love
now we have to tell each other
all we've done
it's not easy
but at least the worst is over

## I Know

You see it was the summer before third grade
and before my memories started to fade
I was aware and I was afraid

I followed along
I played their game
I didn't know it would ruin my name
I didn't know I'd never be the same
I was too young to know
too young to grow
but now I know what they've done

Now I know how much it broke me
but they don't care
they laugh
and it chokes me
they don't care for the impact
they just wanted it in the moment
I'll never know why they did that
I know they'll never own it

My life changed forever that day
I'll never know what I could have been
my body's been damaged, too drenched in sin
oh my what my life could have been

It feels as if something's always lingering
something that I'm hiding
no one I can confide in
see me lying just to hide my crying
you see me laugh but it feels like I'm dying

Someone creeping around the corner
they'll say "I tried to warn her"
those clothes she wears
but the truth is it doesn't matter
life isn't fair

# BAD ADVICE

I can see the truth
I don't need to show proof
I can feel it in my mind, my veins, my core
I could go on more
but I don't have to
because I know

98

## CHILD IN DESPAIR

Like a child in despair
I couldn't grow until I became aware
the darkness within
is where it all begins
a light inside started to burn
igniting a will to live
I finally knew what I had yearned
to be what I always needed to be
the person I was meant to be
I started to feel again

## The Future

I'm drowning out this evil sound
I won't let them push me down
I know in the end I'm hell bound
but I won't let it keep me down
whatever comes from my defeat
I'll rise through the fire on risen feet
because I've seen the future
and all it brings
a golden sun on a hillside run
cathedral ceilings and diamond rings
it doesn't make sense
but it's what I've seen
I've seen the future
and all it brings

## ROCK GODS

When I was a little child
I lived in denial
I grew up not knowing what to do
I still don't really have a clue

now I'm just dreaming
of the day when it will all be gleaming
hoping and praying with the Rock Gods
the bells will be ringing
come on angels keep on singing
joking and playing to the Rock Gods

Now I'm on a roll
all those long nights, they'll take their toll
party hard till we're old
come on now give me all your gold
now that we're on a fucking roll

I'll just be dreaming
of the day when it will all be gleaming
hoping and praying to the Rock Gods
the bells will be ringing
come on angels keep on singing
joking and playing to the Rock Gods

### DIVIDE & CONQUER

Divide the parts that made me love you
Divide what kept me holding on
Conquer all the fears inside me
Conquer what kept me holding on

## THE DANCE

Sit down
Stand up
Relax
Freak out
Believe

Sit down
Stand up
Relax
Freak out
Dance

Sit down
Stand up
Relax
Freak out
Breath

## It's Okay

It's okay to feel
It's okay to reel
It's okay to reel in all the feels
It's okay, it's okay
It's okay to feel insane

## OLD SCHOOL LOVE

We got that old school kind of love
the kind you never give up
the kind that can get kind of tough
but you work it out
because you grew around the hood
and all your friends
have always been the same
and if you broke up
the whole family breaks
and if it ended you would end
and that's not how this story ends
we're in it till the end

# BAD ADVICE

# THE END

## ME

I've shed so many tears
I've had so many fears
It's become clear
This is what it's like to be me

# ABOUT AUTHOR

Sara L Ward lives in North Carolina with her husband and their two children. Along with this collection and others, Sara also writes children's books and fantasy novels. When she's not wrangling her own children and working her day job, she enjoys doing several other creative things, as well as hanging out with family and friends. Life is rough but pleasant.